ANCIENT GREECE

BUILDERS, CRAFTSMEN & TRADERS

Jane Shuter

Heinemann Library
Des Plaines, Illinois

03 02 01 00 99
10 9 8 7 6 5 4 3 2 1

Library of Congress Cataloging-in-Publication Data

Shuter, Jane.
    Builders, craftsmen and traders / Jane Shuter.
        p.   cm. -- (Ancient Greece)
    Includes bibliographical references and index.
    Summary: Introduces the work of artisans responsible for the buildings, statues, and carvings of ancient Greece; describes the lifestyles of the people; and indicates the importance of traders and trading.
    ISBN 1-57572-736-6 (lib. bdg.)
    1. Greece--Civilization--To 146 B.C.--Juvenile literature.
2. Building--Greece--Juvenile literature. 3. Artisans--Greece--Juvenile literature. 4. Greece--Commerce--Juvenile literature.
[1. Greece--Civilization--To 146 B.C. 2. Building--Greece.
3. Artisans--Greece. 4. Greece--Commerce.] I. Title. II. Series:
Ancient Greece (Des Plaines, Ill.)
DF77.S465   1998
938--dc21   98-18530
                                                                     CIP
                                                                      AC

Acknowledgments
The Publishers would like to thank the following for permission to reproduce photographys. Alinari-Giraudon p. 21; Ancient Art and Architecture Collection pp. 5, 7; Ashmolean Museum p. 23; British Museum pp. 20, 28; C.M. Dixon p. 22; Hirmer Fotoarchiv p. 19; Metropolitan Museum of Art, New York pp. 17, 26; Royal Ontario Museum p.11.

Cover photograph reproduced with permission of the Ashmolean Museum.

Every effort has been made to contact copyright holders of any material reproduced in this book. Any omissions will be rectified in subsequent printings if notice is given to the Publisher.

Any words appearing in the text in bold, **like this**, are explained in the Glossary.

CONTENTS

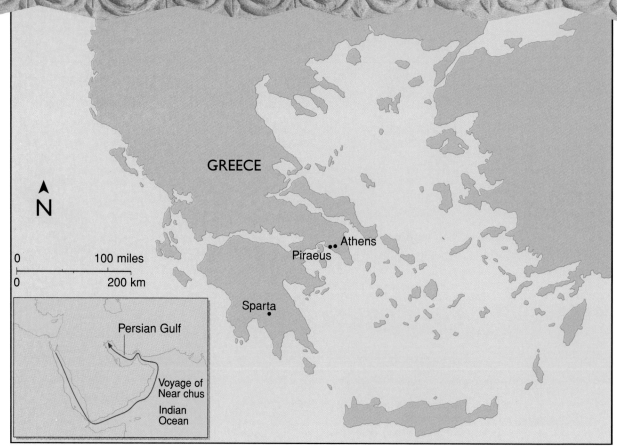

Ancient Greece

BUILDERS

Ancient Greek builders made **temples** and huge statues out of stone with very simple tools. They made ordinary houses with mud brick. Few of these have survived for us to see now. They have crumbled away or have been built over.

Timeline

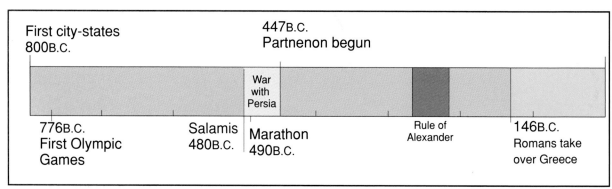

First city-states
800B.C.

447B.C.
Partnenon begun

War
with
Persia

776B.C.
First Olympic
Games

Salamis
480B.C.

Marathon
490B.C.

Rule of
Alexander

146B.C.
Romans take
over Greece

CRAFTSMEN AND TRADERS

Some Ancient Greek cities, especially Athens, were large. There were many **craftsmen** living in the cities who made things like pots, statues, boots, and vases. Some **goods** that craftsmen made, especially the pottery decorated with scenes from everyday life, were in great demand in other countries.

Merchants were important, too. They traded goods from the **city-states** for things that the **citizens** needed. They usually needed food, like **grain** for bread. They traded with city-states and with Greek **colonies** in other countries.

Many modern buildings, like the British Museum, in London, England imitate styles of the Ancient Greeks.

Builders used stone to build the most important buildings in a city. They used stone for **temples**, theaters, public baths, and the buildings around the **agora**. This was the main square in the city.

BUILDING TOOLS

Builders did not have machines to dig and flatten the ground or lift things. They needed a lot of people to help. Pulleys and ropes were used to lift things. Most heavy work, such as hauling stone, was done by **slaves**. Aristotle, a Greek thinker, called slaves "a tool that just happens to be alive."

BUILDING RULES

The Ancient Greeks thought things were more beautiful if they looked balanced. So they thought the best kind of temple was a rectangle with matching porches on the front and back and the same number of columns along each side. Its length, width, the width of the columns, and the spaces between the columns were all carefully calculated to have the same **mathematical ratio**.

The Parthenon in Athens. The building was begun in 447 B.C. and was finished in 432 B.C. The carving and decoration took six years to complete.

The Parthenon is a huge **temple** built to honor the goddess Athena. It was built between 447 and 432 B.C. It was built almost entirely with **marble**. This was very heavy, expensive, and hard to move. Blocks were cut to size at the **quarries**. The temple is covered with carvings showing scenes from stories about the lives of the gods.

THE COST

The Parthenon cost a lot to build. It cost about 12,000,000 drachmae. A builder could earn one drachma a day and a sailor could earn half of a drachma. A **slave** cost about 100 drachmae.

A GREEK WRITER DESCRIBED SOME OF THE PEOPLE WHO WORKED ON THE PARTHENON:

Carpenters, model makers, coppersmiths, dyers, stonemasons, workers in gold and ivory, painters, embroiderers, and engravers. Also carriers and suppliers of materials—merchants, sailors, wagon makers, drivers. Also rope makers, weavers, leather workers, road builders, miners. Each craft also had its own group of laborers to pick up and carry.

Building the Parthenon

The Greeks decorated their **temples** and public buildings with stone carvings. They also made beautiful statues mostly from **marble** or **bronze**. A statue of the goddess Athena, about 33 feet (10 meters) tall, was at the center of the Parthenon. It was made by Phidias, who was famous for his huge statues. First, Phidias made a wooden frame. Athena's face, arms, and feet were made from carved ivory. Her eyes were made from precious stones. Her long dress, helmet, and shield were made of gold. They were all carefully fitted onto the frame.

PHIDIAS—A THIEF?

Phidias' enemies accused him of keeping some of the gold from the statue. Luckily, he had made the pieces of gold removable. He took the statue apart and weighed the pieces in public. He showed that he was not a cheat. Then someone pointed out that Phidias had put himself and Pericles, an important man in Athens, in the picture of a battle on the statue's shield. He was accused of not showing the goddess enough respect. He left the city and went to work somewhere else.

This is what Phidias' statue of Athena probably looked like. It is a modern reconstruction in a museum.

Important Greek buildings were made from stone. What about ordinary workshops and homes? These were made from mud bricks on a stone base. The bricks were so crumbly that burglars were called "wall piercers."

It is very hard to tell what an ordinary street in Athens looked like. A visitor at the time described the streets as narrow and winding and the buildings as old and needing repair. There are no better descriptions. Homes in Athens have crumbled away and have been built over many times. There are some abandoned towns in other parts of Greece where the stone bases of houses remain. These buildings give us clues about Athens.

HOUSES

Most Ancient Greek houses were built around a courtyard. The windows and doors were small. Each home had a part of the house for the women and a more public part for the men. The most important room in the house, the **andron** (where men ate and gave parties), sometimes had a tiled floor. Other floors were made of beaten earth.

A residential
street in Athens

Piraeus was the **port** of Athens beginning in 493 B.C. As Athens became more important, Piraeus became a town itself. There was a paved road with protective walls on each side that ran the 3.9 miles (6.2 kilometers) from Athens to Piraeus to keep the road safe.

WHAT WENT ON IN PIRAEUS?

The Athenian **navy** kept their ships at Piraeus. It was also a big **trade** port with docks for ships and warehouses for the **merchants**. It had meeting places, shops, workshops, **temples**, and theaters. Its public baths were deep enough for several people. (Most public baths were small, so people scooped water over themselves.)

NOT ALWAYS GUARDED

The walls between Athens and Piraeus and the walls around Piraeus were pulled down in 404 B.C. when Sparta beat Athens in a war. Spartan generals watched the walls come down while girls played music on flutes to celebrate such a big victory. The walls were rebuilt in 393 B.C. when Athens was strong enough to disobey Sparta.

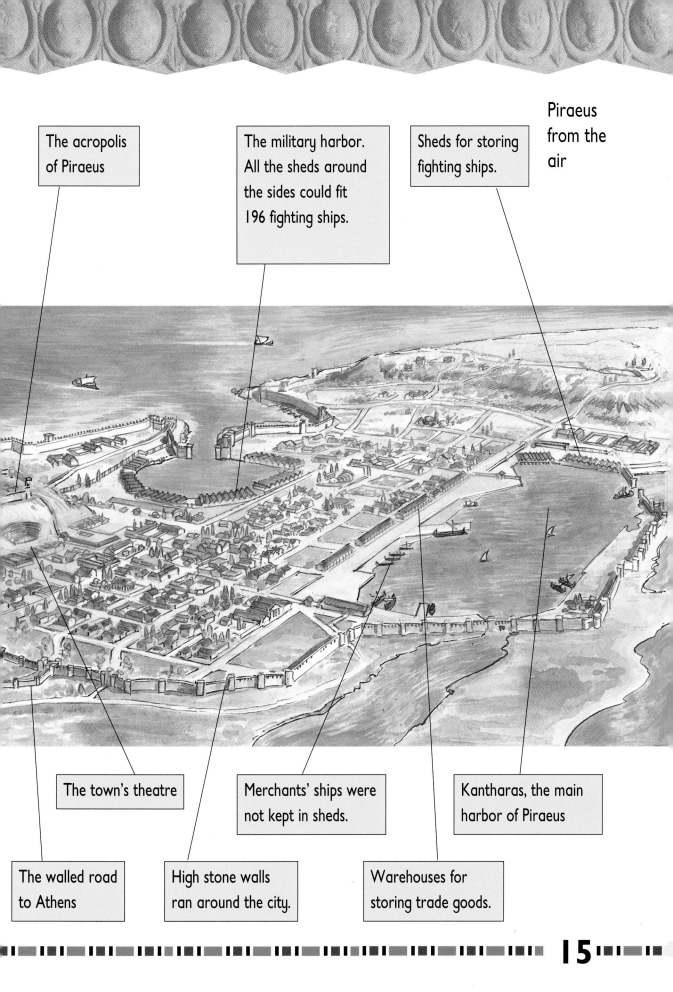

The acropolis of Piraeus

The military harbor. All the sheds around the sides could fit 196 fighting ships.

Sheds for storing fighting ships.

Piraeus from the air

The town's theatre

Merchants' ships were not kept in sheds.

Kantharas, the main harbor of Piraeus

The walled road to Athens

High stone walls ran around the city.

Warehouses for storing trade goods.

Trade was very important to the Greek **city-states**. They did not grow enough food to feed everyone, so they had to trade to get food. City-states also traded to get **goods** like tin (which they needed but could not mine in Greece) and luxury goods such as silk cloth and glass bowls. They traded with other city-states, with other countries, and with **colonies**, places in other countries where Greek people lived.

Places where various Greek city-states traded

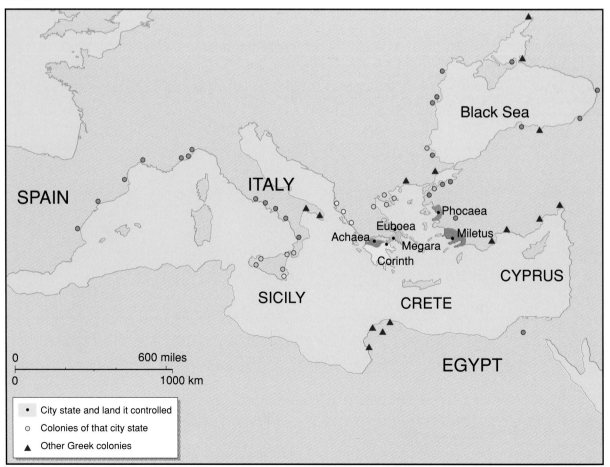

City state and land it controlled

Colonies of that city state

Other Greek colonies

WHAT DID THEY TRADE?

The Greek city-states all made enough wine and olive oil to trade. Some city-states were also famous for other things. Miletus made very soft, fine woolen cloth. Athens made pottery decorated with black and red scenes from stories about the gods and everyday life. Greek traders traded different things at different places, depending on what those places needed and what they had to spare.

These **merchants** are weighing goods on a large balance scale.

TRADING WITH EGYPT

Greece had a lot of silver in the ground that could be mined. Egypt had very little silver, but most years it had more **grain** than it needed. These things made a good trade. They were not the only things Greece and Egypt traded. Egypt traded carved ivory and linen cloth for Greek slaves or olive oil.

Merchants could make a lot of money by trading. But they took risks, too. They often lost ships full of **goods** in bad weather. The writer Hesiod warned: *Go to sea, if you must, only from June to September—and even then, you are a fool to go!*

CHEATING THE BANK IN 360 B.C.

Not all shipwrecks were due to bad weather. Many merchants borrowed money to **trade**. Banks often agreed that if the ship sank they would not ask for the money back. Some merchants tried to cheat the banks. A ship owner named Hegestratos and his agent, Zenothemis, sent a ship full of goods to Marseilles. They signed a document saying it was loaded with **grain** for Athens. In fact, it was empty. About two days from land, Hegestratos made a hole in the ship and leaped overboard. But he could not find the small escape boat and drowned. Zenothemis tried to get everyone to leave the ship by saying it would sink. But they stayed on board and got the ship to land. People could see that it was empty and that they had tried to cheat. The bank took Zenothemis to court, which is how we know the story.

This pot shows how important trade could be to a country. The ruler of Cyrene (a Greek colony in North Africa) is supervising the packing.

JUST ONE TRADING SHIP

Archaeologists found the wreck of a trading ship from about 350 B.C. near Cyprus. They figured the ship was about 49 feet (15 meters) long and had one sail. It was carrying wine from Rhodes, millstones for grinding corn from Kos, and almond nuts from Cyprus.

The weather was not the only danger for trading ships. Pirates were a danger, too. Their ships were faster than trading ships. Trading ships were built to carry a lot of cargo, not for speed.

This vase painting shows pirates attacking a trading ship.

Piracy was not seen as bad and was a way of life for many people, as long as they obeyed the rules! These included not raiding ships from countries or **city-states** that were friendly with their part of Greece.

FISHERMEN

Pirates and traders had bigger ships, but most of the ships at sea were fishing boats. Fishermen had small, shallow boats that could move easily around rocky shores and islands. They fished with nets and also caught lobsters in wicker pots.

A carving of the goddess Athena helping the adventurer Jason get ready for a voyage

EXPLORING OTHER SEAS

The Ancient Greeks were careful sailors. They sailed by day, landed at night and always tried to keep land in sight. They did explore, looking for new places to settle in and **trade** with.

NEARCHUS

Alexander (356–323 B.C.) was the first ruler to lead many **city-states**. In 325 B.C., he sent a captain named Nearchus with about 1,000 ships to explore the Indian Ocean. The huge waves were a shock because they were used to the calmer Mediterranean Sea. The men were very seasick! They sailed to the Persian Gulf, digging through sand bars and landing to find food. They often had to fight for it. At last, they reached the Persian Gulf. Alexander was glad to see them, as he feared they had drowned. A Greek historian said, "Their hair was long and neglected, their bodies filthy and shriveled."

CRAFTSMEN

All Greek cities had **craftsmen** who made different things. In some cities, especially Athens, there were many different crafts. The craftsmen worked in small workshops of ten to thirty workers. People who made the same things often had workshops in the same part of the city. A craftsman earned about one drachma a day. This was twice as much as an ordinary workman, who earned only enough to live on.

IN ABOUT 414 B.C., ARISTOPHANES, A GREEK WRITER, DESCRIBED THE BUSTLE OF A MORNING IN ATHENS:

When the cock crows at dawn, they all jump up and rush off to work: the bronzesmiths, the potters, the tanners, the shoemakers, the bath attendants, the corn merchants, the lyremakers, and the shieldmakers. Some of them even put on their sandals and go when it is still dark.

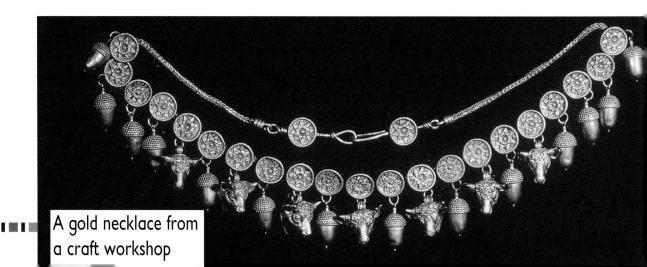

A gold necklace from a craft workshop

SMALLER CITIES

Smaller cities did not have such a wide range of craftsmen as Athens. There were not as many people, and they were not as rich. They bought less expensive luxuries and lived more simply. A craftsman had to do many different jobs to make a living.

This shoemaker is cutting out a child's shoe. His tools are on the wall. He has water in a large bowl because wet leather is easier to cut.

In about 300 b.c., the Greek writer Xenophon described the good thing about people having special skills:

In small city-states, the same man makes beds, doors, plows, tables, and even builds houses too. It is impossible for a man who works at so many crafts to be very good at all of them. In a big city-state, there are enough people for a man to make a living from one craft. In some places, one man cuts shoes and another stitches them up.

Pottery containers were important for storing food, oil, and drink. People ate from pottery plates and dishes. They drank from pottery bowls and cups. Even small villages needed a potter to make everyday things. Most pottery was quite plain. But the most famous Greek pottery is the decorated pottery, which was mainly from Athens. Museums today have more of this pottery on display because it is so beautiful, but potters would have made more of the plain kind.

ATHENIAN POTTERY

The Potter's District of Athens was near the river. The clay the potters used had a lot of iron in it, so once it was baked, it became a reddish color. Athenian vase painters used black as a contrasting color. They painted detailed scenes of everyday life and also scenes from stories of the time about gods, goddesses, and heroes.

Historians think the smaller cups and dishes cost between one and two drachmae and the bigger pots and vases between two and three drachmae. Very well made and decorated pots could have cost more.

A pottery workshop in action

Greek women lived separately from men. Most Greek homes had private rooms at the back of the house for the women. The only public rooms were at the front of the house and were used by men to entertain each other. The **andron**, a room used for male dinner parties, had a separate door to the street, so visitors could come and go and not bump into the women of the house.

These women are spinning and weaving.

GETTING MARRIED

Girls were married off by their parents, usually between 14 and 18 years old. Many girls never met their husbands before. In a play by Sophocles, written in 430 B.C., a woman says:

> When we come of age, we are thrust out of our homes away from our families. Some of us go to strangers' houses, some to foreigners' homes. Some houses are joyless, others hostile. Yet, we are forced to praise our home and say that all is well.

Spartan women hardly ever saw their husbands. The men lived separately until the age of 30 and only visited their homes secretly from time to time.

ATHENS

Athenian men who could afford it kept their wives and daughters shut up at home. Well-behaved women were not supposed to go out except for public festivals. Husbands or servants went shopping. Women stayed at home, spinning wool and weaving cloth.

HOW DO WE KNOW ABOUT THEIR HOMES?

EVIDENCE FROM THE TIME

Most brick-built houses have crumbled away. In some places, like Athens, they are buried under modern houses. But some stone bases of the houses have survived.

These bases can tell us the shape of ordinary homes. We know they had tiled roofs because tiles have been found nearby.

Doors and window shutters were wooden, as in this vase painting. Wood was scarce. When people left their homes during wars, they often took their doors and shutters with them!

FURNITURE

Compared with many people now, the Greeks had few possessions. When a rich Athenian was arrested, his goods were listed and taken away. So we know he had 2 chests, 11 couches (Greeks ate lying down), 4 tables, 1 sofa, 5 chairs, 1 bench, 2 clothes chests,

NEW EVIDENCE

Archaeologists can find out new things each time they **excavate** a new place. In 1966, they excavated a farmhouse in the country at Vari. They figured out what the farm would have looked like. They also found pottery beehives. This was the first real evidence that the Greeks kept bees in beehives to make honey. They did not just collect wild honey.

The farmhouse at Vari probably looked like this.

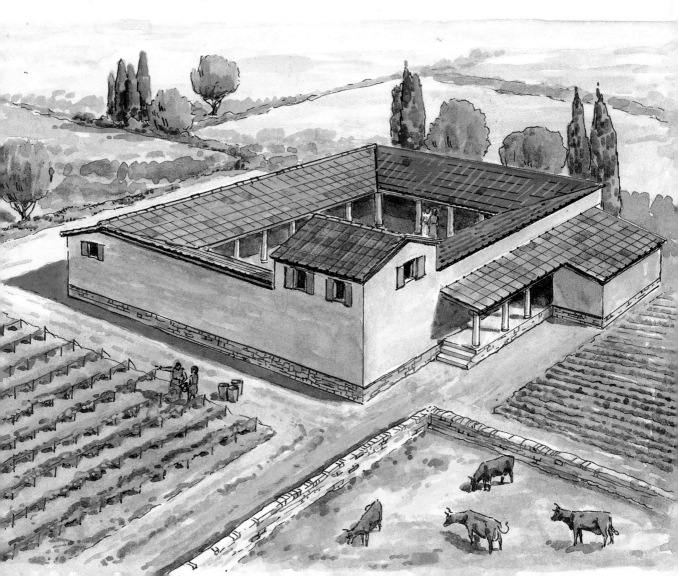

agora an open space often near the center of a town with public buildings and shops. It was often used as a meeting place.

andron the room in a Greek house where men met for dinner parties

archaeologists people who dig up and study things left behind from past times

bronze a metal made by melting tin and copper together

citizens a person born in a city to parents who were citizens. A citizen had rights in their own city that they would not have in another one.

city-state a city and the surrounding land it controls

colonies places set up in one country by people from another country

craftsmen men who have been specially trained to make things such as shoes or pottery

excavate when archaeologists excavate, they dig down through the ground layer by layer and record all the things they find

goods things that are made, bought, and sold

grain types of grasses with fat seeds that are eaten. Barley, wheat, rye, oats, and rice are all grains.

marble a stone that is very hard and heavy. It can be polished to be made very smooth.

mathematical ratio where measurements balance each other. So, if a temple is 7 yards meters) wide and 14 yards (meters) long the ratio of width to length is 1:2 (7 divides into itself once and into 14 twice). The Greeks then used this ratio for other temple measurements. So, a column would be 1 yard (meter) wide and the gap between columns would be 2 yards (meters)

merchants people who buy goods in one place and sell them at a higher price in another

navy ships used to fight for a country

port a town by the sea where ships can land

quarries places where stone is dug out of the ground

slaves people who are treated by their owners as property. They can be bought and sold and are not free to leave.

temple a place where gods and goddesses are worshiped

trade this has two meanings: a job, for example, "Shoemaking is his trade."; or selling or swapping goods, for example, "Greece traded oil for grain."

MORE BOOKS TO READ

Millard, Anne & S. Peach. *The Greeks.* E D C Publishing. 1990.

Pearson, Anne. *What Do We Know about the Greeks?* New York: Peter Bedrick Books, Inc. 1992.

Sauvain, Philip. *Over Two Thousand Years Ago in Ancient Greece.* New York: Simon & Schuster Children's. 1992.

Wright, Rachel. *Greeks.* Danbury, CT: Franklin Watts Inc. 1993.